Vivien Jones lives on the north Solway shore in Scotland. Her short stories and poetry have been widely published and broadcast on BBC Radio 4 and Radio Scotland. Her first themed collection of short stories, *Perfect 10,* was published in 2009 by Pewter Rose Press.

Her first poetry collection, *About Time, Too,* was published in 2010 by Indigo Dreams Publishing. In 2010 she won the Poetry London Prize, her work chosen by Michael Longley. She was awarded a Writer's Bursary from Creative Scotland for *White Poppies* (Pewter Rose Press, 2012), short fiction on a theme of women amongst warriors.

She regularly leads writing projects for new writers and is currently a Literature Animateur in Dumfries & Galloway. She is one of three editors of the region's literary journal.

www.vivienjones.info

Vivien Jones has a sharp eye and a sharp ear. She is fascinated by the magic and the mystery of craft and art. Her own consummate craft shines through every poem in this collection. These beautifully observed poems are full of music and insight into the joy and sadness of being human.

John Burns, past editor of *Cencrastus,* writer and critic

The best poetry sharpens the reader's awareness and perception, and Vivien's writing achieves this across a diverse range of topics – reflections on time and its passage, love and loss, the joys of the natural world, the dense particularities of craftsmanship ... and many more. She brings to her work an empathic, humanising and sensuous intelligence, alert and insightful, and lanced by wit and humour. This is a richly rewarding collection.

Angus MacMillan, literary editor of *Southlight literary journal*
a published poet in Gaelic and English

Short of
Breath

Other books by the author

Hare (erbacce, 2008)
Something in the Blood (Lapwing, 2008)
Perfect 10 (Pewter Rose, 2009)
About Time, Too (Indigo Dreams, 2010)
White Poppies (Pewter Rose, 2012)

Short of Breath

Vivien Jones

Cultured Llama Publishing

First published in 2014 by
Cultured Llama Publishing
11 London Road
Teynham, Sittingbourne
ME9 9QW
www.culturedllama.co.uk

ISBN 978-0-9926485-5-8

Printed in Great Britain by Lightning Source UK Ltd

Jacket design by Mark Holihan

Contents

Music

Detritus

You waved by the car,
that last time:
see you soon, I'll phone.
No caption on the moment
to say fix your face now
because you will phone
to say, *sorry, a bit sore,*
and that was the last time
before today.

Your DNA is on our recorders,
sorry about that, you laughed,
your saliva now our treasure.
What was that last harmony,
an end-of-piece chord,
three notes that made us smile?
What of the luter's detritus: strings, music,
chamois, pencils, erasers, footrest
and tuner,
that creative mess at your feet,
even at concerts.

rise,
sit,
kneel,
bell rings
respond,
sing,
reflect,
pray,
your shell in a box.

Somewhere in my mind
your perfect plucked note pierces
through; a memory of shared bliss
in a wood lined palace,
a lute in your hands,
sound rushing along passages,
up chimneys, a floor away
I hear a note and its decay,
part of your essential detritus.

Skittle Alley, Greenwich

The photo freezes us,
four strangers drawn
to a vacant music room,
blissful as the chord ends.
Musicians all, lovers of
Renaissance music and viols,
we arranged ourselves
by personality; bass,
tenor, alto and soprano people,
equal to the task.

We do not know each other,
like each other, share politics
religion, newspapers or place.
But when we play, since
we have fine-tuned our guts,
the bows catch the strings,
fingers dance on the frets.
Since the music is well within us,
we are, momentarily,
blessed, elevated, brilliant.

The photo freezes us,
four friends now, having
shared musical intimacy.
We exchange names, postcodes,
plan a holiday stopover,
even though we doubt
it will, or should, happen.
Ecstasy can't be planned,
instead, we confine to memory
an unexpected moment unparalleled.

Bonnie Sweet Robin
to comfort Colette

They carve your name
in the oak you felled.
The acid chips on bench
and floor take a day
to accumulate, a day that
stirs up memories,
an oak-strong kinship
with your wife.

We visit, we walk through
a dreamed world made real.
So even though we did
not yet know you,
in the new laid paths
that touch the house
and working places,
we know the beauty
of your dream.

Hey Ho, the Mavis*

Sibelius software, I'm working on
a Tudor song transposed for viols,
worktop under a fan of manuscript
containing a song as urgent as
the one sounding on my rooftop,
where a thrush, head thrown back
is stating his intention of making
the very perfection of nests

*Scottish thrush

6

All Yews Blues

in 2009, Miles Davis's Kind of Blue was 50 years old

Woke up this century,
germination so slow,
a single poison seed
wrapped in a scarlet aril,
shat by a bird to lie still
for a year or more.
Then the freeze,
the cracking husk,
back to back cotyledons
reaching for the light;
and all that time.

Woke up this morning,
session in mind, nine hours
in two days to germinate
a music haiku, pared down,
to brave essentials,
my jazz fevered fingertips
slowed, in seeking
the mood of now.
I kind of feel
this may be a moment
that is a birth.

A yew, a meditation in wood,
can live three thousand years.
1959 – fifty years of cool,
Fifty – just a babe.

Layperson's Science

Pluto in Three Moods

Pluto's Lament
134240 in the minor planet catalogue

I am untouched,
no spacecraft has squatted on
my impossible surface,
processed
my impossible atmosphere
fleetingly gas at perihelion,
frozen nitrogen,
laced with methane,
feeble microbars
fail to keep a grip.

The ninth planet,
since dwarfed.

I am cold,
unobserved for millennia,
discovered in error,
someone didn't do the maths,
someone else thought
me and my moon, Charon,
were one, no-one knew
his tiny sisters,
Nix and Hydra,
until Hubble peered.

The ninth planet,
since dwarfed.

I am dark,
too far for light to lift

my rocky heart,
what warmth I know
is just less cold.
Neither day or night
rolls across my face,
silence, true absence,
beats no time
through my existence.

The ninth planet,
since dwarfed.

Pluto's Adolescence

I don't care what you say,
if I want my equator to point north,
it's up to me, and if that means
my pole points to the sun – tough.

And don't try and tell me
my orbit is eccentric – if I want
to pass in front of Neptune,
you can't stop me.

And you can tell that gang of moons,
Io, Europa, Ganymede, Callisto, Titan, Triton,
and Moon (duh!) just because they're bigger then me,
it doesn't mean a thing – you can scrub me

from your astronomical maps,
you can call me a 'dwarf' all you want,
un-naming me does not get rid of me,
I won't wear rings like Saturn,

or get fat and gassy like Jupiter,
I will spin in my cold darkness,
not listening to anything
but the pounding music of the galaxies.

Pluto's Hope

I am to be flown past,
A New Horizon,
ten years heading
like a dart, but sleeping,
at 34,000 miles per hour,
reporting, each week,
only a little awake –
'I'm still here'.

On July 16th 2015
6000 miles above me,
so close I may hear it
click, hum and suck
my data, my being.
Its telescopes, particle detectors,
its radio waves, its spectrometer,
its infra-red mapping eye
will gaze across my surface.

They worship knowledge
The New Horizon ones,
they will display their images
like trophies, on bright screens,
coloured and given voice.
They will simulate my being,
make me familiar, beautiful,
they will say my name many times,
make themselves famous.

They could restore me,
the ninth planet.

Small Time

I think I'll have a water-clock –
a *Clepsydra,* a water thief,
a measured pot full of water
with a hole down low, and
a wax disc to stop the flow.
A clock for small events,
just like the Greeks, I could time
my speeches in the law courts
(a large pot for large crimes)
or my visits to the brothel
(have to watch the wear and tear)
The soft song of flowing water
could keep me company in tasks
too short for the calendar.

Big Time

*the distinction between past, present and future
is only a stubbornly persistent illusion.*
Albert Einstein

Measuring time is a practised art.
Dynamical, measuring the rhythms
of stars and sunsets.
Atomic, measuring the minute
pulses of atoms and molecules,
yet definition eludes us.
Time snaps at the heels
of our life, even the lines just read
are inexorably gone. Yet we persist
in taking memory for a clock
when it is just a receding echo.

Only the night sky allows us
the reality of the past.

What Time is it?

I'm cooking scones,
twelve minutes in a hot oven,
time enough to hang out the washing,
or wash the dishes, or feed the cat,
or phone my son to say hello.

Seven hundred and twenty seconds
in twelve minutes,
two thousand million, and counting, in my life,
the scones will change from raw dough
to lightweight delight – and me?

The seconds have flown over me,
there must have been special ones
when I first heard Beethoven, fell in love,
my two moments of conception.
There should have been a bell.

There is a buzzer.
Hot, sweet-smelling air announces
the scones are complete.
Out there in the cosmos,
does it matter that I am not ?

Wood and the Making Process

The Elm to the Groundsman

Don't cut me – I'm only late in leaf;
like every elm it takes a long while
to suck sap up my barley sugar ribs.
Chestnut leaves are splayed like
horrified hands, the cherries overdoing
the blossom, but look close
and you will see pairs of leaflets
flying like flags from the twigs
on my rumpled trunk; I'm alive,
just not showing it yet; don't cut me.

On the hill beyond the buildings
I can see the fringe of the forest;
I long for the forest, for undergrowth,
to fight for light with lesser trees.
I'd give up my glorious crown
to tangle branches with a beech
or sycamore, to be scratched by brambles,
I'd even welcome the grip of ivy,
the company of owls and bats and birds
or lovers lying at my feet.

I have heard his chainsaw, its ripping whine,
I have seen a canopy shudder, the arc of its fall,
the empty space created sucking in air.
There are no elms nearby to make him choose
not me, the cherry has stayed squat and florid,
the chestnut brandishes pretty flower cones.
How I yearn to pull my roots from the earth,
limp to the forest, stand among other elms.
A tree, but for its seeds, has no mobility.

Night time, still and cold, the moon
draws black lines behind me. He has
sprayed my trunk with yellow paint,
the same tone as my lichen.
Trentepohlia – my itching companion –
so an end to itching and me.

Carrifran Wildwood
August 2012

So this is how it was.
Beyond this point the notice says
Tread softly as the planters did.
The fence is high, high up the
valley sides, no sheep or goat
can graze the young trees,
as once they finally did.

The flitter of young birch,
the fullness of young hazel,
the low U-form of myrtle,
fragrant in the hand,
orange clusters of rowan berries
dipping in the breeze,
speak of the hundred year future.

The 6000-year past, sealed
in a coat of peat, disgorges
a bow, a hunter's joy,
yew from Rotten Bottom;
was it deer, wolf or bear
he stalked in the dusk,
his knees brushing bracken ?

Tracks run two ways,
from the road to the valley head,
one road to and fro, possible to trace.
But the track through time,
that's another matter –
we're making a museum of land,
no life sustains it now.

Blackwell, above Windermere
On crossing this threshold, we pass into a charmed
territory where everything shall be in harmony
Mackay Hugh Baillie Scott, architect, 1897

Upstairs

We use our Sundays for good works;
like any upright Victorians, we visit
museums and galleries. Today is

Blackwell, above Windermere,
a Manchester mayor's spare home,
a play-piece for an architect,

unlimited funds, unlimited space,
a site on the hill away from the crowd,
a family palace, a hall, a temple.

My socialist soul should be soured, but
in a room wider than a worker's whole house,
I feel only admiration for the honest work

of wood and metal makers. The chairs,
cupboards, tables for living use, testament
to inheritable skill, of time well spent.

Downstairs

The spaces used by the servants did not
contain the same level of decoration...
from the guide to Blackwell: the Arts and Crafts House

There's a floor plan in the guide book;
the east wing, the cold wing, the dark wing,
are where the servants squeezed past
each other, the ancient dance of service
kept well behind a stout oak door,
this wing now made into a café and shop.

There's no floor plan of the attics, bedspace
for folk with no time for aesthetics. Sloping
ceilings, tiny windows, some of which
gave a glimpse of mid-summer skies above Windermere,
but no view at all at the end of most working days,
when dark meant rest and a shivering sleep.

Two Rules for Good Living

I ...and lose his own soul
*For what is a man profited, if he shall gain the whole world,
and lose his own soul?*
Matthew 16:26

*To make it felt that hand-work really does allow expression
of a man's soul and self, and so is worth doing for its own
sake, and worth purchasing even at some cost to the buyer*
Keswick School of Industrial Art, 1898

It's only a bed, single at that, but
ornament straight from the tool edge,
the softening chamfers meeting
in complex geometries, invite touch.

They are only fire-irons, muscular,
tools for a fire lit daily, but tong hands
anticipate touch like a lady pianist
poised to play a light metal tune.

They are only door handles, but
a falling leaf, curved into the palm
its only sharpness, form observed
in a garden planted for inspiration.

They were only Kendal carpenters
carving their rowans and roses
into oak, their preening peacocks
from drawings by urban aesthetes.

They not only looked, but saw.
The worth of their work did not
weigh their pockets down, the men
who took the money took the dross.

II Hand Crafting

To try to displace by hand-work the crude metal
and wooden ornaments produced by steel dies
and hydraulic presses.
Keswick School of Industrial Art, 1898

A simple aim: to understand
how wood cuts, splits, joints,
lies under the plane, peeling ringlets
from the keen swoosh of the blade.

A simple aim: to understand
the fleam and the rake, the kerf debris
of the saw, rip-cutting, cross-cutting,
the tannin bite of cut oak in the air.

A simple aim: to understand
how annealed copper, brass or silver,
hollowed, blocked, raised and planished,
makes a bright, hard, useful vessel.

A simple aim: to understand
the dance of a hammer in the hand,
the shift of weight and angle
that forms the facet, the light-catcher

A simple aim: to understand
the imprint of a man on his work,
to know his tool stroke by its cut,
to credit his God, but his craft too.

Saw Mill
Creca

We took three lengths of beech,
leg-length long, arm-length diameter,
grey skin, barked in satin,
white wood showing,
we end-over-ended them
towards the bedlam shed.

The men and the blades
danced over the wood,
the back and forwards bed
fed the cylindrical lengths
to the spinning blade;
the blade spat boards, just so.

Curve and knot and ripple,
rolling out from the saw
emerge now, even slices;
the men gesture, all speech
swallowed by the mill roaring
at its workload; a screech,

the quick spark of a severed nail,
a saw blade's life shortened.
The men wipe their brows, frown
over a calculation more troubling.
How much to turn a graceful tree
to usefulness – to squares, to blocks ?

Cold Snap

Branches, brittle and silvered,
scrape past each other rasping
a hollow song into the still air.
The path through the icy woodland
beckons.

Sunday families walk their kids,
their dogs running,
out and back, out and back.
Laughter and barks split the air,
woollen scarves like flags waving,
A promise of a tea-time treat
drives numb-fingered children on,
the wood hums,
populous as any Breughel painting.

Grey light shrinking,
the wood darkens.
Three-day frost, turning
again back from the melt,
building hoar-frost towers,
crystal on crystal.
An owl launches in silence
the moment before,
with gunshot bedlam,
the branch snaps.

Yew Trees
Traquair

Lattice canopy, snaking branches,
a fragrant green parasol,
orange heartwood burst open
where weight and gravity snapped
the heavy branches.

The ground is layered with needles,
brown over grey over black,
yielding under my summer sandals,
working between my bare toes,
as I walk the shadow of their growth.

I picture the grain inside,
the wild figures of old yew,
erotic fine line drawings
round sheared-off branches,
almond swellings, she-shapes.

The children dream great ships
in the branches, walkways and masts,
men talk of long bows and legends,
but for you, the instrument maker,
the deep orange fractals
of yew mean a singing wood.

Family

Stocking

Hanging amongst the ivy
dripping over the mantle,
catching on its exploding flowers
smelling of churchyards,
our stockings hang.

I approach, eyes closed by order,
my fingers reach through
whispering wrapping
to pull out a golden sun.
The faint crackle of foil
promises chocolate.

I see my sister has one too.
My thumbnail about to separate the foil,
I have an ivy thought.
I look at the ivy and wish
to be as ivy on the tree,
centipede roots clinging, creeping
onto what seems bigger, stronger.

I slip my chocolate into a pocket,
wait with ivy patience
for my sister to cram her mouth
with sweetness.

Later I will take out my chocolate,
eat it, slow as ivy,
savouring my sister's envy,
punishing her beauty,
taking small revenge.

Short of Breath

After the tearful waking,
we spoon, my little asthmatic and me,
he tracks my breathing, and follows
my rhythm with perfect trust.

Quite quickly, he dozes and
I track his thin breathing, hearing
the whistle of narrowed tubes,
the speeded-up thump of his heart.

I doze against the curve of his back,
he surfaces through discomfort,
whimpers, I stroke, he snuggles back.
I wake again and listen.

Once he is calm, I am calm,
I smell and absorb his warmth
through my belly. They say
it may pass with adolescence.

He is only eight.

Emerald Magic

She had a raincoat of
shimmering emerald green,
in which she twirled,
the body A-shaped,
hem tickling her calves.

Tony-next-door and me
were the Bisto Kids,
copied from the packet,
with rosied cheeks and berets.
I loved Tony.

She shut the bedroom door.
I thought I heard her weep,
then the sigh of scissors,
the clatter of the Singer,
at last, her singing.

Tony and me practised
'Aaaah, Bisto!' in the mirror.
The bedroom door opened.
She teased my little brother
'Has anyone seen Robin Hood?'

She'd cut it to pieces,
transformed her beautiful raincoat
with Singer, scissors and tears,
to a tunic, fringed with triangles,
a hat with pinked green feathers

He won first prize in the under-5s,
Tony and me, the under-10s.
His smile as wide as Sherwood,
in not quite Lincoln green,
but emerald magic.

Dad the Carpenter

I was twelve, just won the Athletics Cup,
when one Saturday I watched him all day
making a box; he said I could
if I didn't stand on top of him,
if I didn't ask questions all the time.
That was hard; I wanted to know
why he pinned and glued it shut.
What use was a sealed box, I nearly asked.
Then he took down his best saw,
drew a line two thirds down, and cut,
and there was a box and lid, perfect.

With the don't touch chisels
he fitted the black hinges,
whistling, focused, blind to me;
I saw the tiny screws grip,
he opened and shut it,
added a tiny hasp.
I dreamed a special present.
Before lunch, he cut a square out of the lid,
took metal mesh from a paper bag,
trimmed it, pinned it,
covered the hole from the inside.
'Breathing space,' with a threatening elbow,
was all he said all morning.

Lunch was oxtail soup and rolls – too hot –
lasting too long, shared with my dancing sister.

I stroked the box's wood-grain sheen.
From the shelf he took a paint-pot,
a pinny, rough gloves, turpentine from a flask,
a paint brush with splayed bristles.

The paint was thick, black, tarry,
the wood grain soon obliterated,
the now black box propped on nail legs to dry.
I sighed - no dreamed-of present, then.

'For my maggots,' he said.

What Remains

I got the Malta album,
mostly black and white photos
and a set of colour postcards.
The black and white photos
spark Technicolor memories,
show an unexceptional family.

The black and white photos
show my parents in love,
glow with light from the sea,
record how quickly we grew,
my sister, already a beauty,
my brother asleep, me, scowling.

The black and white photos
list the cars we hired; The Singer,
The Morris, The Mayflower,
to drive round the island
like well-mannered tourists,
Moorish in long sleeves and scarves.

The black and white photos
have dying glue on the corners;
when they fall out I turn them over
and find my Dad's neat writing,
recording the dates and places,
no need of the names; it's always us.

The only other thing I have,
my Hornby O-gauge clockwork key
for the train set that started my trip
towards my self, aged five, already
truculent, headed for rebellion.
I played alone; I made my own world.

What remains has been distilled by love.
What I see now is that the track was,
and still is, a circle.

Cornwall

Gunwalloe
Late Summer, 2012

The name, the shape on a map,
a legend found on Wiki,
what drew us there was chance.

A steep, stony, snaking path,
only the horizon visible
over the turf on the bank.

The splay of the path edge,
expanding, wide open, the
sudden smashing of surf.

That turquoise glory, weight
of water, deafening, a half mile
of broken waves, slithering.

Deep sucking on pebbles,
sorting them from fine to coarse,
a long rhythm, slither and suck.

Not sand but loose piled pebbles,
our sandals filled and emptied
with each sideways sliding step.

Sun and small clouds belie the legend,
three broken back ships, a notice
says treasure hunting is forbidden.

Except the one you take away,
the photo in the camera,
the picture in your head.

Bronze Age Boat
Falmouth, 2012

Skipper offered a scraper
'to keep it off your clothes'.
Not sure if volunteers
were what he wanted
on his beloved boat.

But I've got my hands on it.
My fingertips are coated
with tallow, stuffing the
shakes in green oak to
stop them drying out.

Tannin bites the air
all round, the chip-chipping
of adzes beats a rhythm
good for working back
and forth across the cracks.

My fingertips speckled
with black oak splinters,
sore in skin softened
by tallow, seven frames*
to caress over and over.

The Skipper smiles,
'Good for your skin'.
He's happy that I cream
his baby's bottom
with my mother's hands.

* frames are grown oak ribs with the form in the limb as it came off the tree, as in cruck cottages

Sconner Games

I am a girl,
but I am nine so I am Tarzan,
my brother is five
but I don't make him be Jane;
he can be Cheetah.
I'm not a cruel child.

The woods are endless,
dark and tall, mossy moist,
the paths only just there.
Hansel and Gretel ambush
Tarzan and Cheetah, any
stranger may be evil.

I take the fraying washing line,
climb the mapped out trunk,
I know the handholds, the places
I can stretch across. I knot the rope,
stifle a fierce need to pee,
shut my eyes and jump.

Cheetah runs for the house,
our agonised parents arrive,
wipe my snotty nose, hug me,
smack me, forbid me. The blood
on my grated knees is a trophy.
My brother starts my legend.

Last Supper
Mevagissey

Bags packed, kitchen swept,
minds already on the way home,
eyes on the clock, just time to catch
the quayside hut if we hurry.

She's in blue overalls, stained, cleaning up,
still willing to stop and say the names
of flat silver-sided fish among the ice.
'This dull brown one is Megrim Sole,

nice with scallops and a bit of samphire.'
A flash in the pan, a shake, a salty whiff,
sweet and steaming, the creamy sea
in my mouth, silk notes dissolving.

We drive away, lose the high-sided lanes
on the motorway, head inexorably north.
A sore gap between memory and the present,
temporarily bridged by fading recall.

In a Changing World

Late Winter Garden
Malta, 1950s

Our apricot tree, bare of leaves
and skulking lizards, stands grey.
Whitewash walls built to throw sun
are dim; sleep stunts the shrubs.
The wet warmth of a Maltese spring
entices mossy things to spread whilst
the pulsing sun does not appear.
But the earth tilts, the sun comes closer,
thin splits on the apricot twig
hint at movement beneath.
The moss cooks, retreats, surrenders,
lizards stir, and so do I.

Instead of Sparrows

It was the first of the wild I ever knew,
the mild scratching of reptile claws,
a panic in the air round their wings,
and the gentle insistence of their beaks.

My sister preferred the gliding swans,
our stale bread in greaseproof wrapping
shared exactly in half, though she argued
that the swans, being bigger, needed more.

My rigid arm extended, a crust wedged
into the curl of my fist, my breath held,
for the descent of worldly wise sparrows,
in chocolate, black and grey elegance.

My stale bread turns green.
But the robins don't flock,
the tits are shy, and
the greenfinches are gaudy,

and the sparrows are few.

Getting Warmer

That memory that my children laugh at,
of long fused days of blue sky summer,
of my own brown legs in shorts,
and white cotton or yellow straw hat.

Remembering holiday games that lasted from morning
until dusk, the rough boys being cowboys,
the soft boys and all the girls being Indians,
the dusty chase from wood to field, hollering.

It's all quite soft edged, illusionary, delusionary.
It must have rained; we must have stayed indoors,
squabbling over Ludo, eating banana sandwiches,
waiting for the soft showers to pass.

I watch from my window, the village children
pass up and down the road, nodding to iPods,
dressed in perfect unison, polite and tribal,
hooded against the day-long rain and conversation.

The beach is no longer a siren call to adventure;
sunshine calls only for sun-block and sunglasses.
Will they too remember the blaze of their childhood,
or has a landscape disappeared ?

Two Plane Journeys
Stansted 2006; London 1954

A palace of an airport hall,
abundant, lavish furnishings
that anyone may sit upon
while they wait.

My grown son approaches smiling,
familiar with passes and processes,
he beckons me towards
a queue, a snake
of other travellers.

A small child wails, infuriated
by delay, his parents' small steps
not enough to soothe.
I find my patience,
remembering…

Fifty years back, a night-time flight,
the rearing eagle on the wet runway,
Mummy all fuss and carrier bags,
brother asleep over one arm,
sister trembling under floodlights.

The judder and roar of the engines,
propellers disappearing in spin,
brakes unlocking, a metallic smell
of fuel and heat, the runway moving.
I swallow, examine the sick bag.

We fly to Italy, we flew to Malta,
the night sky still stunning,
the fractal patterns of cities
larger this time.

No Snow

What shall we do on the Breughel days,
when the scarcity of winter light calls
us to play under the pale fire of the winter sun?

Shall we store our hats and scarves and mittens
in attics, alongside obsolete machines and toys,
to sit quietly waiting for a summons from a museum ?

Will our children gaze at photographs of winter,
when we sledged and skied, as they gaze at our clothes,
with laughter and amazement, looking at another world?

No broken limbs on skidding pavements, no cars in drifts,
no need to feed the old, to check their fuel and health,
there could be good things too, and yet…

what else tastes like snow, what else tingles like cold fingers,
what thrill like the slow slide of a snowball down the neck,
or the grey white whisper of an unexpected snowfall?

Summer is Late this Year

April was no surprise, cool,
breezy, scraps-of-cloud days,
the right amount of promise.
But there were few May mornings
when sun begged the curtains
to part and dazzle my eyes.

In June some fits and starts
that teased, but blew cold
by the time the picnic was made.
A July with warm, unceasing rain,
children's squashed faces on the window,
deprived of chasing on bikes.

But August, August shaded in greys,
a sky of 2B, 3B then 4B pencil strokes,
dove tone to charcoal, saturated.
It is September, trees are turning early,
starved of sunlight, a windy day
rips leaves away – not yet, I cry.

Not yet; I have not stored a vision
of sun to see me through the winter.
Summer has been elsewhere this year.

After Kerouac's *Visions of Cody*

It's 64 years since I was born, but
there's no-one with me here tonight.
My sons making money in cities,
grandchildren intent of growing,
siblings being grandparents –
any one of us might just stop living.
If it was me, my husband
would just come
looking for supper or talk,
with shavings on his clothes,
he would touch my cooling body,
want to ask me what happened,
re-calculate the rest of the day.

If it was him, some sudden stop,
fallen over his work-bench.
I'd be mad that he was late for supper,
march down there practising rage.
Then I would rage – how could he
better demonstrate our togetherness
than by deserting it?

Though it's background most days,
it's been there since the start,
the black side of love is fear of loss,
and one of you is going to get it.

Patna to Sauchiehall Street
on a slow bus from Castle Douglas

The bus picks up no passengers in Patna.
The coal's long gone from tumulated hills,
thin men with starved spirits lean
against the wall of a boarded up institute.
Retrain, skill share, volunteer,
Don't drink yourself to death on our watch.
Wait long enough, you'll come under 'heritage'.
The church, short of faith, echoes with old women
raising small change for 'Our Friends Abroad',
baking buns, jumbling.

Glasgow's something else,
brash, boisterous, brimming with goods.
It is here, walking in Sauchiehall Street,
in the trail of three women,
in primary silks and gold braid,
black, black and black hair.
(Indian, Pakistani, Bangladeshi –
how would I know?)
that three hunters encircle them,
denim warriors, beer-fumed,
roaring, gobbing at their feet,
'Get fucking home – ye cunts!'

They, the women, reach inside,
are still, silent, untouched,
just gathered a little.
I tremble.
They do not.
(Hindu, Sikh, Jainist, Buddhist –
how would I know?)

Their silence steals the spine
from casual malice; the men,
each of them secretly shamed,
run off, laughing.

Why Trees are Sympathetic to Lovers

When you walk the slow walk of lovers
through woodland, hands meshed,
shoulders inclined, speaking nonsense,

your shoes kicking up autumn leaves or
compressing snow, trampling down bluebells
or making summer dust on the paths,

the presence of trees, our tall imminence,
our winter black frames, our summer abundance,
says welcome to the families of creatures

that pair and mate and make young
amongst our many layers,
the insects that teem in our roots,

the others that tunnel our bark,
the birds that forage and bore in our wood,
that nest where branches triangulate.

You are so blessed, you lovers,
who lie between the walls of our roots,
rolling on a sheet of leaves, making babies.

Just accept the grand design – be glad
that genes direct the tallest tree to set tiny seed,
not heaving its roots in passionate motion,

ravishing its neighbour with crackling branches.
We are content to shelter the family of creatures
that are moved to close coupling under cover.

Walking with the Carpenter
Lochwood, near Templand, Dumfriesshire

This oak-wood, this creaking oak-wood,
was full grown all my life,
in time lapse slow-fall on the steep hillside,
nursing rows of ferns on its decayed boughs,
backlit lettuce-green, nodding.

Standing nearly still through world wars,
all Victorian life, all Georgian life, all Jacobean life,
saplings in Stewart days, growing by inches
through seasons of acorns, galls and burrs,
the slowing of sap causing arthritic poses.

We exclaim – look at the twenty year old
sycamore growing out of that bole,
look at the wool skein twist of the limbs,
look at the … look at the …
look at the wood.

You see the table-top, the door, you remind me
my father would have seen the ship's prow, the keel,
that the carpenter would see the cruck, observing
the weight and strength of curved oak wood,
horizontal, defying gravity.

We stroll back to the car, under the canopy,
we speak of ecology, of infant nature study,
and suddenly I remember first seeing you
in our early days, long hair, beard, brown eyes,
looking like Jesus the Carpenter.

from Dumfries and Galloway

Solway Exchange

Criffel said to Skiddaw,
full and clear may be your lake,
as the sun slides down my back
throwing peach light across
the Solway. I send greetings
to your ancient grey eminence.

Skiddaw said to Criffel,
a blessing of bright heathers upon you.
I fall to darkness this hour
but daylight will swathe me
in white mist boas, long before
your black flanks are visible.

Criffel said to Skiddaw,
weight be upon your blanket of snow.
I rise straight from the sea,
no flat marshlands round my feet,
no thousand boots turn me to dust,
I carry no scars of erosion.

Skiddaw said to Criffel,
frost preserve your lace shawl of snow.
But I am legend, muse to poets,
my flanks streaked with pilgrims' feet.
(Very nearly a Munro were I in Scotland,
and you only a little over half).

Criffel said to Skiddaw,
may your peaks be ever higher,
for I provide the gentle slopes
for children and other wild creatures
to roam, a mountain at their back door,
a Saturday stroll with a sweetheart's view.

Skiddaw said to Criffel,
We will be quiet now that sea mists roll.
All along the Solway, white furls
cloak the low ground, cloud fingers
pour down the mountains' rocky grooves.
Invisible, Criffel and Skiddaw fall silent.

Skiddaw (931 m) Criffel (570 m)

Urr, Inhabited

On Loch Urr, grey water stirs,
pike, imprisoned, kills and
charcoal ribbons turn to red.

High in the catchment,
sea trout wreathe silver coils,
the greyback salmon persist

until grey November, spent
of life, dying on grey stones,
gargoyles with undershot jaws.

Above Glenlair, black pools
under trees, playwaters for otters,
cavorting without splashing,

leaving only bubbles and fish bones,
bodies woven in moving skeins,
their beaded eyes glistening.

The Reid Pool divides the water
through stone channels where dippers
plunge, seeming suicidal, rise again

to shake and swallow; the damsels
and dragons on stained-glass wings
in mating finery fuse in the air,

from virgin to corpse in a day,
but for the kingfisher who cuts
across their timetable with a beak

merciless as the pike under a ledge,
watching wild brown trout tangle
in the camouflage reeds, dappled

as any thing in Hopkins, unsuspecting,
as the river monster, hungry as a tiger,
cleaves through cover, trailing ribbons.

Naiad

She is white, wet, naked,
beautiful as needs be;
in the deep shadows of
Crichope's ravine, she slides
in and out of vision.
Movement so fleeting
it might be a reed rustling,
her river-weed hair floats
among leaf-fall and bubbles,
she waits as she always has,
keeper of the running water.
But Naiads and rivers change little,
scooped out rock, pebble swirled,
swollen from winter rainstorms,
all there is to show for great age.
She knows every course it may take,
every pool that overflows to thin rivulets,
over ferns and moss, every new flow.
Her winter garden is decorated with
bright wrappings of crisp packets,
aluminium keys gleaming among ferns,
she must always make the best of it.

Beyond Gatehouse Station

Grikes make clints – it's well known
in geology: a solution fissure will
dissolve limestone into flinty outcrops.
Yet the Clints of Dromore are granite,
free of their glacier some 18,000 years,
lichen rich, adder richer, with slabs
vertical enough to make poets
of the climbers who name them –
Spare Rib; Comfy Chair; Quoth the Raven;
and the one no-one expects,
The Spanish Inquisition.

Mile on mile after rolling mile,
heath and heather, blanket bog,
acid soil attracts the alliterative,
acid soil, short of nutrients, makes
sundew clasp its deadly fingers,
makes butterwort stick to entrap;
insects dissolve, slip down their
velvet, vegetative gullets.
Patchwork sphagnum turns
to peat either side of our lifetimes,
slow as evolution.

Aucheninnes – the Field in the Water Meadow
or **Dalbeattie Dump**

A halo of gulls marks the spot,
where layers of bright rubbish
turn grey in compression, sunk
into Aucheninnes Moss, landfill.

Land over tributary waters,
Little Kirkgunzeon Lane as is,
flowed once on chartered land,
through fields in the water-meadow.

Only place names keep the history:
Armannoch – monks' share,
Ernespie – bishop's share,
12th Century, monastic communities
sprawling out from Whithorn

in between the Nith and the Urr.
Polchillebride – St Bride's Kirk Burn –
named after her church, at the gates
of Aucheninnes or Dalbeattie Dump.

Dispute, denial, dismay, disarray,
a drowned excavator ends the search,
yet Aucheninnes or Dalbeattie Dump
still wears a halo of gulls.

Herons at Powfoot

A heron, in three shades of grey,
the gothic arches of its wings
tickling the waves in slow motion,
drops like thistledown,
uncurling its neck, dropping its legs,
taking three dainty steps, freezes,
a hunting statue, waiting.

A circular high-water pool
made for Edwardian swimmers,
half for men, half for women.
In illusionary moments
the unruffled rising tide
provides an unseen perch,
a ring of birds on water.

A summer feast, when
silver salmon boil in shallow
water, high stepping herons
pick their way to the fattest,
tossing their heads back,
pointing the streamlined fish
down their streamlined gullets.

Dusk, and the squadron
heads back to the reed-bed
to stand, invisible again
through the long night.
A grey, shot-silk carcass
draped by a fish-pond,
the end for one plundering diner.

At the Stewartry Museum
Kirkcudbright

In my Junior class
we had a box of shapes
to fondle, name and remember.
Square, rectangle, circle,
triangle and polygon.

Only later, in geometry,
did I encounter the crescent,
a pair of arcs, Ludo discs,
one hiding behind the other,
best seen in old and new moons.

In the glass case, a bronze circlet
hangs like the moon.
Someone, some quiet craftsman,
in a place without battles,
has taken days to scribe spirals.

Some trader has travelled north,
thrilled the nine tribes with
metalwork: swords and circlets.
A Celtic warrior, looking to mate,
has fondled the bronze and bought

it for the woman in his chariot.
He rings her neck with bronze,
she traces the curve to the break,
feeling the space at her nape,
not quite a ring, not yet a shackle.

Literal

CCTV

In this window,
look at your reflection,
your winter self
in padded coat and boots,
you pause to read me
and I read you back,
through this glass I steal your face.
Looking is not a one-way process,
always, my lens looks back,
but you don't notice me
noting your pausing,
your passing.

Literal

From graffiti in a rural bus shelter

A municipal man has ordered
that the honest grey concrete
of my rural bus-stop be painted
with an infant palette to show
that, over the hill, lies a bright
blue sea with red-sailed yachts.
It lies; over the hill lies a
grey mud shoreline and no boats.

Inside the bus-stop the legend
of Murphy who thrives on cock
speaks across the pee-smelling floor
to the jelly fish prozzies and
someone else, who is fat as fuck,
has listed her favourite food.
It's true; the spirit marker tells
of people larger than most lives.

Graffiti Tales

Characters from a rural bus shelter, since erased

Murphy and Shanks are headed for town
looking to catch up with the Spoons Boys.
Shanks loves their style – Levis and lace –
Murphy just loves their bums,
peach plump in tight denim.
He's looking for a bus shelter,
breathing in damp concrete
and piss stain while he gropes.
Murphy thrives on cock.
He's bi though – not averse
to tilting his taste towards one
of the Jelly Fish Prozzies
if the Spoons Boys are elsewhere.
Bella, Queen of the Prozzies, is his favourite,
huge, the kind of woman
who proclaims her size like a blunderbuss.
'I like chips, beans, pie and cheese
and I am Fat as FUCK.'
She's advertising her appetites,
lots of everything. No restraint.
Murphy thrives on his own cock in her company.
Shanks, though, is aw to fuck.
One of the Spoons Boys has come on to him,
he doesn't know how to keep face –
doesn't know how to say 'I just like watching'
to the pretty boy before him.
He looks round in desperation.
Murphy might intervene and scoop the prize
but Murphy is deep in Bella's cleavage
on the other side of the pub.
He doesn't look inclined to surface
in the near future.

When Shanks heads for the bog,
he is followed by a smirking Spoons Boy.

88 – Two Fat Ladies – a Saga

J & J, Jane and Janine,
88 – two fat ladies, well cut hair,
one platinum in parts,
the other purple as grapes,
take turns at the phone.

'This is J & J Hair Salon,
how may I help? '
They learnt the spiel
at college after school,
chums from Infants.

Janine is the cutter,
scissors gleaming, clicking,
never a false line,
never a shake,
too skilled to shampoo.

Jane is the people's friend,
half the town's Christian names
in her address book head,
'Back or forward?' she asks
before the washing begins.

Her hands make scalps tingle,
the flexing of fingers causing
something like orgasm. She asks,
'Conditioner?' They'd let her
do anything to prolong things.

Janine's chat is ambitious,
away from soaps and quiz shows,
more from the news, or a drama,
clipped from the BBC usually,
anything but politics.

Jane plays it safer,
'Been your holidays?'
and tells small tales
of her own adventures.
She's been to Ibiza twice.

They both dance in flat shoes
(On your feet all day, the college warned)
Small slip steps round the chair,
never out of reach of dryer,
sprays, razor, comb, mousse,

rollers in neat rows, arranged
in sizes for sets and perms,
colour charts for tinting –
'this one's called Medusa,
quite dramatic, isn't it ?'

Janine asks, 'Isn't that
something to do with snakes?'
Some documentary tickles her
memory. 'I don't like snakes;
never watch David Attenborough'

Jane replies, dancing on,
'What about this one – Salome?'
J & J inspect the chart;
their client looks from one to the other.
'Better with your usual,' they nod.

Jane consults her address book head
'No word from Mrs Davies'.
Janine looks up, scissors still,
a rare solemn moment.
'She died – Mrs Clay told me.'

Jane considers, edits,
'Cancel those appointments
then, and the order for lacquer.
She was the last to want lacquer –
they don't like stiff these days.'

Janine giggles, 'You said stiff
and Mrs Davies is dead – sorry.'
Jane stiffens. 'You don't have
to make smart remarks all the time.'
Janine turns away, to hide her grin.

Jane takes her own unused scissors,
looks at Janine's broad shaking back,
plots the point where she might
still that clever tongue forever;
the plague of her schooldays.

The doorbell rings, Jane is distracted,
the moment passes, Janine unaware
of circumstance in the person of Mrs Clay,
averting a Greek tragedy. Jane smiles,
takes her coat, 'Back or forward today?'

Maryhill Shops

Now we've got the bus pass
Glasgow is a breeze; we park
in Spence Street and toddle
down the hill for an 18 bus
to the Byres Road, via Maryhill.
Hissing and rocking in the rain,
it scoops us up and barges into
the middle lane like Davy Coulthard
on a good day – when he was good.

We've climbed the swaying stairs,
bagged the front seat off cursing
schoolkids, peered through the window
at the shops, netted like hen houses.
Spewing out of the bookies
come the old men in suits and trainers,
heading for a lunchtime kebab.
Meet the wife at the hairdresser's
before an afternoon in Tesco's
upside-down castle on Maryhill Road.

Close to the turning for town,
we glide into the right hand lane
close by two lurid police cars
parked all which ways outside the bank.
Or is it the chippie – hard to tell
when they're all secured by bars
as if someone might steal chips.
But here, the price of his chips,
you'd have to take out a mortgage.

Or is it that wee estate agent
next to the baby shop, by the launderette
in that line of shops that still display
the names of long dead proprietors
in Maryhill Road.

Beverages

My hands make brackets
around this warming mug.
Through the rising vapour
I look at the café crowd
and wonder, which one
has just left a lover, which
will return to a happy home,
which one has lost a job,
which one might be my friend.

Do you remember in Geography
those Technicolor pictures,
the five great continents?
Do you remember India, a place
of elephant and temple, terraces
where lovely ladies in saris,
red spots on their foreheads
plucked aromatic tea leaves?
Sip slowly and remember.

I only drink coffee these days.
Tea makes me think of my mother
tied up in an apron, shoogling
the brown betty, warming its belly
before the scatter of black confetti
and the cascade of boiling water
that produced a fragrant cloud.
She would have loved this café,
its Assam and Darjeeling airs.

Eating with Vickie and Peter

Out of the earth,
thirteen green stalks,
this morning's harvest
due to be blanched,
drenched in butter
and with eyes shut,
sucked.

Acknowledgements

Some of these poems have appeared in print anthologies: *Dactyl, New Writing Scotland, Pushing Out the Boat, Abridged* (Eire), *Meniscus* (Australia), *Heart Shoots*. Other poems have been a part of performances with music, whilst some others have been published on www. poetsonline.org; glasgowtosaturn.com; www.poetandgeek.com; www. inksweatandtears.co.uk

Cultured Llama Publishing

hungry for poetry
thirsty for fiction

Cultured Llama was born in a converted stable. This creature of humble birth drank greedily from the creative source of the poets, writers, artists and musicians that visited, and soon the llama fulfilled the destiny of its given name.

Cultured Llama is a publishing house, a multi-arts events promoter and a fundraiser for charity. It aspires to quality from the first creative thought through to the finished product.

www.culturedllama.co.uk

Also published by Cultured Llama

Poetry

Notes from a Bright Field by Rose Cook
Paperback; 104pp; 203x127mm; 978-0-9568921-9-5; July 2013

Sounds of the Real World by Gordon Meade
Paperback; 104pp; 203x127 mm; 978-0-9926485-0-3; August 2013

Digging Up Paradise: Potatoes, People and Poetry in the Garden of England by Sarah Salway
Paperback; 160pp; 203x203 mm; 978-0-9926485-6-5; June 2014

The Fire in Me Now by Michael Curtis
Paperback; 98pp; 203x127 mm; 978-0-9926485-4-1; September 2014

Short stories

Canterbury Tales on a Cockcrow Morning by Maggie Harris
Paperback; 136pp; 203x127mm; 978-0-9568921-6-4; September 2012

As Long as it Takes by Maria C. McCarthy
Paperback; 166pp; 203x127 mm; 978-0-9926485-1-0; February 2014

Anthologies: poetry and short stories

Unexplored Territory edited by Maria C. McCarthy
Paperback; 112pp; 203x127mm; 978-0-9568921-7-1; November 2012

Lightning Source UK Ltd.
Milton Keynes UK
UKOW07f0741181214

243343UK00007B/161/P